Unraveling the Endless Knot

Unraveling the Endless Knot
©Sandra Noel, 2019

No part of this book may be reproduced by any means known at this time or derived henceforth without written permission of the publisher or author. The exception would be in the case of brief quotations embodied in the critical articles or reviews and pages where permission is specifically granted by the publisher or author.

Books may be purchased in quantity and/or special sales by contacting the publisher. All inquiries related to such matters should be addressed to:

Middle Creek Publishing & Audio
9167 Pueblo Mountain Park Road
Beulah, CO 81023
editor@middlecreekpublishing.com
(719) 369-9050

First Paperback Edition, 2019
ISBN: 978-1-7332163-3-3
Printed in the United States

Cover Art: Summers Bohenstiel
Cover Design: David Anthony Martin
Author photo: Linda Zahava

Unraveling the Endless Knot

Sandra Noel

Middle Creek Publishing & Audio
Beulah, CO

Unraveling the endless knot

*In Buddhism, the endless knot is represented as a
closed symbol
overlapping without beginning or end.
It indicates continuity as the underlying balance of
existence,
a closed circle of cause and effect.*

Unraveling the endless knot
Table of Contents:

1. The missing vocabulary of the divine
2. The Gap
3. One
4. Here, after
5. In the wetland
6. Coming to rest
7. Skagit valley blues
8. Winter song
9. My vocabulary in dreams
10. Mukai Pond before the rains
11. Pileated woodpeckers
12. A thousand moons
13. Following the drift
14. Root and branch
15. Sweetgrass harvest (Skokomish Estuary)
16. Ghost Mountain, Mount Rainier
17. Fire and light
18. The last migration
19. Albatross
20. Crossing the Wallace Line
21. Blue crow butterfly
22. Unraveling the endless knot
23. Flying foxes
24. The wave of forever

The missing vocabulary of the divine

In Inuit there are over 50 words for snow.
Will they melt syllable by syllable
with the ice caps
float among the icebergs
with stranded starving polar bears
sift letter by letter
between empty ribcages
and eye sockets?

*Will there be 50 words for loss
when we are finally done?*

The gap

The pond has loosened
her yellow lily skirt
let it float back down
into the dark water
green leaves
curling brown on the edges
still dance above
in a light breeze
as if moved by music
conducted
by the barn swallows'
looping flight.

Redwings
flash crimson shoulders
and young wood ducks
are on their own
the weak
already line
the osprey's nest
her chicks fattened
on their flesh have flown
and here I sit again
letting the wider world spin
slowing the wheel
finding the gap.

One

Beetle wings pulsate
to the rodent rhythm heartbeat
of a vole underground.

In the pond's center, a heron
bright yellow eye diverted
by my presence.
Beneath his reed shadow
a school of minnows
slip quickly down into the muck.

Silken threads overhead
catch my coat
tearing loose the delicate symmetry
of an orb weaver's work.
In a moment she begins
to digest and spin
the damaged threads anew.
Nothing here is wasted.

It is easy to see
in this beautiful chaos
how we are all connected
wing to heart, leaf to root
predator to prey.

But beyond these green boarders
we cannot hear, cannot see, cannot feel
how one touch of the web
changes everything.
So much is formed and reformed
without our notice.
So much we notice
is only an illusion.

Here, after

I have always kept
a gnarled and knotted belief
in the extraordinary
voices rising lifting
over the low hills
over the small homes
in a place as far from here
as I could run.

The music still plays
the voices still ring
as they did at your memorial
but these will not be at mine.
If there is a coming together
afterwards
I hope it is birdsong
my son's guitar
the sound of water
of rain.

In the wetland

Reeds are dying down to brown chaff
fountains of white seed pods
float on a light breeze.

This is the golden time
the time of folding in and under.
It has been a hard year.
I welcome dormancy
and a long winter's sleep –
this of course is not possible.

I'll go back to the world in a while
but now the red-wings are out
and if I am very lucky
no one will come down the trail
without feathers or fur
until the sun is well overhead
and it is time to go.

Coming to rest

In the old tool shed
among the rusted rakes
and empty paint cans
field mice have taken up residence
sure the owner has abandoned it
are bold, build their nests in the open
spiders belay overhead on silken threads.

It once held a hundred useful things
for gardening, fixing a broken wheel
a missing shingle, a child's toy.
I think civilization on the downturn
will look like this
overgrown with neglect
coming to rest at last
as nest and shelter
for small, wild things.

Skagit Valley blues

It must have been October
when clouds of snow geese filled the sky
their epic migration from Northern Siberia
ending on farmers' fields.

Well into the day we walked along the single road
towards your home near Conway
watching the great birds gathering
covering fallow fields
with their white wings and conversations.

I think we must have talked about it
how the geese traveled thousands of miles
how cold drove them to this temperate climate
how we were not birds of a feather.

Winter song

There was a song
whistled by the thrush
learned early
and passed on to me
as I stopped by the cattail cloister
thick matted with dead stalks and leaves
of this long, dry summer.

It is the last refuge in the pond.
Golden maple and willow leaves
cover the ground leaving skeletal branches
and no place to hide but deep in the mud
if you happen to have gills
or the cattails, if you don't
but fear the heron's sharp eye
or the hawk overhead.

The song must be of winter
the coming cold and damp
the end of abundance
and time to fly south
if you happen to have wings
or hunker down, if you don't.

My vocabulary in dreams

Call it languid
think of water in the morning
before sunrise
before the osprey
nothing has unfurled
not a wing
not a flag
and ribbon rolls of light
opened by the first feathered seeker
the first mark on newly fallen snow
or blood drops
before the first scream.

Mukai Pond before the rains

A mosaic of dock and soft rush
burreed and wapato
exposed through the long dry summer
waiting for the rains to come
and cover every leaf and stone
for the dragonflies and darners to return
many colored dabblers and divers
and the geese in their black and white attire
the chorus frogs
singing in the season of darkness to come
as the pond rises and widens
we watch the days begin to shrink
bring in the lawn chairs
think about a fire.

Pileated woodpeckers

Bright flash of red
behind an alder snag
the Tat! Tat! Tat!
of avian demolition
echoes throughout the forest
large birds busy with living
excavating grubs
in the pulpy wood
or impressing a mate
beak ringing on the metal gate
at the park entrance
leaves a Braille love note
I wish I could read.

A thousand moons

Moon jellies dance
        a pulsing polka
in time with the tides
        round like their namesake
glow phosphorescent
        a thousand moons
in the dark water.

Following the drift

From this beach
the shore bends to the will
of diurnal tides in the Salish Sea
that roll past our small island
driving drift and debris onshore
where we wander and wonder
the dog and I
at crab parts and plastic pieces
so similar in color and frequency
though one will eventually
succumb to wind, weather and tide
the other remains long past its usefulness
if it ever had any.
The dog's interest and mine
are curiosity
but I do not taste or chase
just observe, sometimes collect,
my pockets are always full.
Sometimes sand sifts
through my dreams.

Root and branch

Cedar roots
    lace the trail

washed bare by heavy rains
    and an early thaw

look like the veins
    in my wrists

as I reach up for a branch
    step with care

not to damage what seems
    to pulse beneath my feet

overhead
    a great tower of life.

Sweetgrass harvest (Skokomish Estuary)

On the estuary at low tide
a woman nearing ninety
in waders and a baseball cap
stops to show me
how to snap the slender stems
with my fingers
her own gnarled as cedar roots
from decades
of breaking, bending and weaving
the tall salt-tolerant plants
into beautiful, useful things
decorated with the dye she extracts
from berries, leaves and roots.
She is an elder and an artist
one of the 'The Big River People'
she has taken me into her reed world
for this small time
her eyes dark and mystical as a crow's.

Ghost Mountain, Mount Rainier

5 a.m. on the dock
and to the southeast
Tahoma, *Mother of Waters*
rests on the horizon
snow-covered clavicle of ice
jutting out over the bay
lights from refineries
glow in the distance
rotting glaciers
down to stone.

Fire and light

The heron sounds
like an old man dreaming
I see his silhouette
against the night sky
until the last veil lifts
and he rises
but like an old man slowly
with protestations
until his broad wings
catch and sweep effortlessly
into a blood red sunrise
created by fire
eating half the state
east of the mountains.

I am grateful to live
on the Salish Sea side
where only ash particles dance
against the sky
no smoke
no fire
just light.

The last migration

There are multitudes
of bright souls on the wing
on their way north or south
depending on the season
depending on the latitude
gliding overhead
in V-formations
their mission is peace
seeking a place to rest.

But where the great plains welcomed
now a drought has wiped away
even the chaff
and to the east, the forests are on fire.

Still wings come
but fewer and fewer each year
until the day when we look up
and see only empty sky.

Albatross

The eyes go first
plucked out, snapped down
as she rises off the heaving sea
squid tentacles twisting, airborne
a feast devoured on the wing.

Arch-winged grace
gliding, patrolling the crosswinds
glowing phosphorescence below
shimmering constellations overhead
touching earth just long enough,
to mate and brood her young
land-bound and vulnerable
clubbed almost to extinction
to stuff our downy pillows
full of oceanic dreams
of endless voyages
becoming poetry
becoming song.

Silver-winged angel
carrier of sea souls
moon-minted thin blades
slicing through the Arctic night
a scythe of fire at sunrise
Icarus ascending, defying the Gods
then dissolving, disappearing
into gray-white day
metamorphosing
becoming myth
becoming dream.

Crossing the Wallace Line

A full moon spills her silver light over the bay.
Buton Beach is glittering with sea shells
and plastic trash.
Brave fishermen in small outriggers
bob like toy boats too fragile to survive
the dark wave shadows rolling in
from an off-shore typhoon.

I am just a visitor here
without the necessity of bravery
but trying to fit in, to be easy
because I cannot think of another place on earth
I would rather be than under these stars
on this island where Wallace drew
his imaginary line
and creatures born in evolutionary isolation
still struggle to survive until the next fire
the next desire for hardwood or hard-ons
more land or bush meat.

With palm frond pen
I draw a line in the sand
between perfect shell and plastic lighter
as if I could stop what is coming–
the great grinding wheel of greed
rolling over forests, beaches, species.
So many others have tried and failed
the line is broken a thousand acres a day
and so they leave, having done (almost) nothing
learning only to love what they cannot save
and living with that hard truth every day, every day
but trying anyway.

Blue crow butterfly

Wings a microcosm
of an immense sky
brief as night
they are one species
only one
on this remarkable earth.

If you think about it
really think about it
it would humble us
it would make us
caretakers
not just takers.

Unraveling the endless knot

Sulawesi flying foxes
are returning to the forest
in a river of night sky
following the scent
of eucalyptus and banksias
on the warm winds
blowing seaward
towards their island reclaimed
at least for the time being
because a man is paid
to put away his cruel snares
but next year may be different.

This year Coho salmon are returning
to a small restored stream near Seattle
renewing their natal journey broken
for a hundred years
yet somehow they return again
following a genetic map
of scent to source
from a thousand miles of ocean
silver to red fire up a river
and home again, at least this year
because a company is paid
to leave its land undeveloped
but next year, or the next
may be different.

Flying Foxes

An old friend
drunk one night in Seattle
when I asked
if she wanted to go downtown
to a bar and hear some music
said bars were places
where people go to hang
upside down like bats.
I never forgot that–
even after the two of us
stopped speaking
to one another
for twenty years.

The last bats I saw
were hanging out on Bat Island
in Sulawesi, Indonesia–
flying foxes, thousands of them
left at dusk to feed on rainforest nectar
and returned to the island at dawn.
As I watched their silent shadows
pass overhead
I was reminded of her words
and our friendship marred perhaps
by too much of every damn thing –
alcohol, drugs and pretty, useless men
too much sweetness in the night.

The flying foxes on Bat Island
were all killed last year
for the illegal bush meat trade.
It makes me want to call her up
go downtown together
and hang upside down a while.

The wave of forever

The cold feels clean
my breath evident
walking over the rise
towards the valley of the firs.
If I close my eyes
the cold creeps into my bones
asking for more
but I am not ready to answer
though somehow
with your quiet passing
it does not seem mysterious.

We live and we die
the deer carcass beside the road
an old cedar stump.

Through the crystalline fields
diminutive marsh wrens rise like a shout
disturbed from their cold retreats
by my passing.
We are a small ripple
through the great wave of forever.

Acknowledgments:

"One", Flying foxes," *Finishing line Press chapbook,* Into the Green
"Albatross", *Barnwood International Poetry Magazine*
"Crossing the Wallace Line," *Hip Pocket Press,*
"Unraveling the endless knot," *Albatross #26*
"Winter song," "The wave of forever", *The Avocet: A Journal of Nature Poetry*
"Blue crow butterfly," *Three Birds Dreaming: An anthology of poetry dreamed one day at a time*
"The missing vocabulary of the divine," *Fredericksburg Literary and Art Journal*

About the Author

Sandra Noel works as a free-lance illustrator, graphic designer and interpretive writer developing award-winning environmental education posters, brochures, exhibits and interpretive signs. She also contributes her artistic and design skills as a volunteer for several non-profit conservation organizations. Her poems have appeared in Pontoon, Protest Poems, Buddhist Poetry Review, Outside In Literary and Travel Magazine, Elohi Gadugi Journal and others, and three chapbooks intitled, "The Gypsy in my Kitchen," and "Into the Green," Finishing Line Press and "The River," Kelsay Press.

For more about Sandra and her work, visit: www.noeldesigninterp.com

ABOUT MIDDLE CREEK PUBLISHING

MIDDLE CREEK PUBLISHING believes that responding to the world through art & literature — and sharing that response — is a vital part of being an artist.

MIDDLE CREEK PUBLISHING is a company seeking to make the world a better place through both the means and ends of publishing. We are publishers of quality literature in any genre from authors and artists, both seasoned and as-yet undervalued, with a great interest in works which may be considered to be, illuminate or embody any aspect of contemplative Human Ecology, defined as the relationship between humans and their natural, social, and built environments.

MIDDLE CREEK's particular interest in Human Ecology, is meant to clarify an aspect of the quality in the works we will consider for publication, and is meant as a guide to those considering submitting work to us. Our interest is in publishing works illuminating the Human experience through words, story or other content that connects us to each other, our environment, our history and our potential deeply and more consciously.

www.ingramcontent.com/pod-product-compliance
Lightning Source LLC
Chambersburg PA
CBHW070210100426
42743CB00013B/3124